# Unseen and Unheard: Recognizing Adult Inattentive ADHD

Amanda Payton

Copyright © 2024 Amanda Payton

All rights reserved.

ISBN: 9798879431650

# DEDICATION

This is for all the people who grew up thinking there was something wrong with them. To all who have journeyed through life feeling out of step, misunderstood, or alone in a crowd—this is for you. To those who grew up believing there was something inherently wrong with them, only to discover their unique minds simply dance to a different rhythm. Your struggles do not define you; they illuminate the resilience and unparalleled perspective you bring to the world. May you find in these pages understanding, solace, and the beginning of a new narrative filled with hope and self-acceptance.

# CONTENTS

| | | |
|---|---|---|
| | Introduction | i |
| 1 | **Chapter 1: The Basics of Inattentive ADHD** | 1 |
| 2 | **Chapter 2: Symptoms of Inattentive ADHD in Adults** | Pg # |
| 3 | **Chapter 3: The Impact on Daily Life** | Pg # |
| 4 | **Chapter 4: Understanding the Diagnosis of Adult Inattentive ADHD** | Pg # |
| 5 | **Chapter 5: Moving Forward with Inattentive ADHD** | Pg # |
| | **Conclusion: Walking Your Unique Path with Adult Inattentive ADHD** | Pg # |

# INTRODUCTION

Welcome to "Unseen and Unheard: Recognizing Adult Inattentive ADHD," a guide that embarks on a journey into the quieter, less visible side of Attention-Deficit/Hyperactivity Disorder (ADHD)—a condition that powers the lives of many like an unpredictable engine. Often overshadowed by its more noticeable counterparts, the inattentive subtype of ADHD navigates through life's waters with a subtlety that belies the challenges it presents.

ADHD is a voyage that starts in childhood and for many, continues into the vast ocean of adulthood. Despite being a widespread companion to millions, the inattentive form of ADHD remains a shadowy figure, eluding detection and understanding. This leaves countless individuals trying to steer through their daily existence without a map to decipher the complexities of their experiences.

In the spectrum of ADHD, we find three main manifestations: the predominantly inattentive, the predominantly hyperactive-impulsive, and the combined types. Our focus here is on the inattentive presentation, marked not by a surplus of energy or impulsive actions but by an internal struggle to anchor attention, organize life's demands, and see tasks through to completion. Its symptoms, often cloaked in the guise of forgetfulness or indifference, demand a closer look to appreciate the full scope of their impact.

This ebook is a lighthouse for those navigating the foggy waters of inattentive ADHD. We aim to illuminate the intricacies of living with this condition, acknowledging the hurdles while also celebrating the unique strengths and capabilities it brings. Our mission is to foster a shift in the way society views and interacts with the ADHD community, advocating for an environment that recognizes and nurtures the diverse talents of all its members.

Reflect for a moment on the essence of living with inattentive ADHD, captured poignantly by someone who experiences it firsthand: "Everything in my life is like skipping rocks on a pond. I can toss myself out there but I only just skim the surface then jump onto the next fire to put out. I am unable to truly dive in deep and finish a task." This sentiment, echoing the feelings of many, highlights the perpetual challenge of engaging fully with the world, a testament to the need for deeper understanding and support.

Considering the vast number of adults potentially navigating life with ADHD—up to 347.6 million worldwide, based on current estimates—the urgency for a paradigm shift becomes clear. The rigid norms of the past no longer serve our evolving, diverse society. It's time for us to expand our
horizons, embracing a more inclusive approach that values the neurodiverse spectrum in all its forms.
"Unseen and Unheard" is not just a book; it's a call to action, an invitation to join us on a journey of discovery, empathy, and empowerment. Together, let's explore the silent spectrums of adult inattentive ADHD, creating waves of change that ripple through the fabric of our society, ensuring that no one remains unseen or unheard.

This is book 1 in a series. "Silent Spectrums: The Spectrum of Adult Inattentive ADHD" is a groundbreaking series designed to shed light on the nuanced and often misunderstood world of adult inattentive ADHD. Through a collection of meticulously researched and compassionately written ebooks, this series embarks on a journey into the silent spectrums that color the lives of adults navigating the challenges and strengths of inattentive ADHD. Each volume delves into different facets of the condition, from identifying symptoms to exploring strategies for daily management, professional growth, personal relationships, and mental health.

"Silent Spectrums" serves not only as a guide but as a beacon of understanding and validation for those whose experiences have long remained in the shadows. Whether you're seeking to understand your own mind, support someone you love, or simply explore the diverse experiences of adult ADHD, this series offers valuable insights, practical advice, and a message of hope and empowerment.

# CHAPTER 1: THE BASICS OF INATTENTIVE ADHD
## Understanding the Quiet Side of ADHD

Inattentive ADHD is like navigating through life with a foggy windshield. This subtype of Attention-Deficit/Hyperactivity Disorder is characterized by a consistent pattern of inattention and distractibility. It's not about refusing to listen or failing to understand instructions; it's more about an internal struggle to keep the mind anchored. Individuals with inattentive ADHD often seem lost in thought, disconnected, or even sluggish. They might find organizing, sticking to tasks, and maintaining focus to be Herculean tasks, especially when the activity demands a long stretch of mental engagement.

## Core Traits: The Invisible Struggle

- **Drifting Focus:** Holding attention on tasks or play feels like trying to grasp water; it just slips through.
- **Overlooking Details:** Small mistakes in work or daily tasks become frequent unwanted companions.
- **Organizational Hurdles:** Planning and organizing tasks feels like navigating a labyrinth.
- **Mental Stamina:** There's a tendency to shy away from tasks that demand continuous mental effort.
- **Lost Essentials:** Items necessary for tasks and activities have a way of disappearing like magic.
- **Distraction's Pull:** External noises and events easily divert attention.
- **Forgetting the Routine:** Daily tasks are often forgotten, leaving a trail of frustration.

# Unseen and Unheard: Recognizing Adult Inattentive ADHD

## Inattentive ADHD vs. Its Counterparts

What sets inattentive ADHD apart is its quiet nature. Unlike the hyperactive-impulsive type, bursting with energy and spontaneous decisions, or the combined type, which blends both sets of challenges, inattentive ADHD is largely an internal battle. This internal focus often means it flies under the radar, leaving many without a diagnosis. The absence of outwardly disruptive behaviors can lead to mislabeling individuals as simply unengaged or lazy.

## Busting Myths and Clearing the Fog

Let's dispel some myths that cloud our understanding of inattentive ADHD:

- **Myth:** ADHD is just a childhood phase.
    - o **Reality:** It's a lifelong journey for many, shaping their daily experiences and challenges.
- **Myth:** Just push through it.
    - o **Reality:** It's a neurological condition, not a lack of effort or willpower.
- **Myth:** It's the 'easier' type of ADHD.
    - o **Reality:** The struggle might be less visible, but it's equally challenging, impacting learning, self-worth, and social connections deeply.

Unseen and Unheard: Recognizing Adult Inattentive ADHD

## Self-Assessment Quiz: A First Step

Wondering if inattentive ADHD might be part of your story? This quiz can be a starting point for understanding your experiences. It's not about diagnosing—only a professional can do that—but it might help you decide if seeking an evaluation makes sense for you.

1. **Daydreaming Dilemma:** Do you find yourself frequently lost in thought, missing out on conversations or details?
2. **Task Tango:** Is jumping from one unfinished activity to another a common dance for you?
3. **Forgetful Flair:** Are you known for being the one who's always misplacing things or forgetting commitments?
4. **Procrastination Predicament:** Do tasks requiring a lot of thought feel like mountains too high to climb?
5. **Misplacing Mysteries:** Is keeping track of your belongings a constant challenge?
6. **Distraction Dance:** Do you find your mind wandering off at the slightest external interruption?
7. **Instruction Interruptions:** Does following through on instructions or completing tasks feel like a puzzle with missing pieces?

## Scoring: Reflecting on Your Journey

If you nodded along to four or more questions, it might be a signal to delve deeper into your experiences with a healthcare professional. Remember, this quiz is just the beginning of a conversation, not the final word.

## CHAPTER 2: SYMPTOMS OF INATTENTIVE ADHD IN ADULTS

Wading through the day-to-day with inattentive ADHD is akin to trying to catch smoke with your bare hands—frustrating and seemingly futile. This chapter peels back the curtain on the everyday realities of living with inattentive ADHD in adulthood, laying bare the primary symptoms and the subtler, often overlooked challenges that accompany them.

Into the Symptoms, We Go!

### The Challenge of Keeping Focus
For adults with inattentive ADHD, zeroing in on tasks, particularly those that are repetitive, lengthy, or not immediately gratifying, is like trying to listen to a whisper in a storm. They may find themselves drifting away during discussions, unable to stick to tasks at work or home, or hopping between activities without seeing them through to the end.

### The Hurdle of Following Instructions
Grasping and holding onto instructions is like trying to catch a wave; it's a complex dance of listening, understanding, recalling, and executing. Adults with inattentive ADHD often find this dance especially tricky. Key details might slip through their fingers,

# Unseen and Unheard: Recognizing Adult Inattentive ADHD

instructions might be forgotten as soon as they're heard, or they might get sidetracked, leaving tasks and projects in a perpetual state of incompletion.

### The Maze of Disorganization and Forgetfulness
Living spaces and schedules can turn into labyrinths of clutter and chaos. Forgetfulness might manifest in misplaced items, overlooked appointments, or missed deadlines, straining both personal and professional relationships.

## Unpacking the Sub-Symptoms

### The Procrastination Puzzle
Procrastination in adults with inattentive ADHD is not about laziness but often stems from a fear of failing, feeling overwhelmed by tasks, or struggling to start on something that doesn't have an instant payoff. This leads to a vicious cycle of putting things off and mounting stress.

### The Enigma of Low Motivation
Finding the drive to tackle day-to-day tasks can feel like an uphill battle. Without the lure of immediate rewards, mundane activities can seem like insurmountable obstacles, fostering avoidance and a nagging sense of underachievement.

### The Time Management Tango
Poor time management is a signature move. Adults with inattentive ADHD might often misjudge the time needed for tasks, struggle to decide what to tackle first, or consistently find themselves running behind schedule, hampering productivity and the ability to meet obligations.

## Embracing the Full Spectrum

Recognizing the wide array of symptoms, from the well-known to the hidden, is crucial for those suspecting they might be dancing with inattentive ADHD. The manifestation and impact of these symptoms can vary greatly, underscoring the importance of a professional

## Unseen and Unheard: Recognizing Adult Inattentive ADHD

evaluation for a precise diagnosis and a customized approach to management.

It's also pivotal to understand that inattentive ADHD doesn't always come solo; it can be accompanied by other conditions like anxiety or depression, further complicating the landscape. Seeing these symptoms in the light of one's overall health and life is the first step toward seeking effective support and strategies for navigating adulthood with inattentive ADHD.

This chapter is not just about listing symptoms; it's an invitation to see through the lens of inattentive ADHD, to understand its impact on daily life deeply. Recognizing these signs in oneself or others is the gateway to pursuing diagnosis, treatment, and ultimately, carving out a path to a more organized, fulfilling existence.

# CHAPTER 3: THE IMPACT ON DAILY LIFE

Inattentive ADHD is far more than a challenge of staying focused or keeping organized; it's a pervasive influence that echoes through the corridors of personal relationships, career paths, and the inner workings of self-esteem and mental health. This chapter delves into how inattentive ADHD intricately weaves itself into the fabric of everyday life, shedding light on its extensive impact and fostering a deeper empathy and support for those navigating these waters.

## Personal Relationships: Navigating the Intimate Terrain

The journey through personal relationships with inattentive ADHD can often feel like walking a tightrope. The pitfalls of forgetfulness and disorganization might lead to missed anniversaries, forgotten commitments, or neglected conversations, potentially leaving loved ones feeling overlooked or unimportant. The difficulty in maintaining focus during interactions can further strain connections, as friends and family may feel undervalued. Yet, within these challenges lie opportunities for deeper understanding and connection. Strategies for stronger bonds include:

- Implementing reminders for significant dates and promises
- Openly discussing the realities of ADHD, inviting loved ones to understand your world
- Engaging in activities that foster connection and presence

# Unseen and Unheard: Recognizing Adult Inattentive ADHD

## Career Paths: Finding the Right Fit

For adults with inattentive ADHD, the professional environment can sometimes feel like a labyrinth. Staying on task, avoiding the trap of procrastination, and managing time effectively can be overwhelming, impacting job satisfaction and the potential for advancement. This can also influence perceptions of dependability and skill among colleagues and supervisors.

Acknowledging that traditional full-time roles may not be the best fit for everyone, especially for those with more severe forms of inattentive ADHD, embracing a portfolio of part-time positions can provide a more suitable and fulfilling career path. This approach allows for flexibility, shorter task durations, and a diversity of engagements. Key strategies for career satisfaction include:

- Leveraging organizational tools and technologies for task management
- Breaking larger projects into smaller, more manageable pieces
- Communicating with employers about potential accommodations to improve productivity

## Self-Esteem and Mental Well-Being: The Inner Journey

Among the most profound effects of inattentive ADHD is its impact on one's inner self. The ongoing struggle with daily challenges can lead to feelings of inadequacy, frustration, and self-doubt, while societal stigma surrounding ADHD may exacerbate feelings of isolation or misunderstanding. Over time, these can contribute to additional mental health challenges, such as anxiety or depression.

Nurturing mental well-being is crucial:

- Seeking support from mental health professionals for coping strategies and emotional support
- Finding community with others who share similar experiences, offering validation and strategies
- Practicing self-compassion, acknowledging the challenges faced are due to neurological differences, not personal failings

## Moving Forward with Awareness

Understanding the broad impact of inattentive ADHD on daily life is the first step toward more effective management and advocacy for oneself. Recognizing the unique challenges in personal and professional realms, as well as the significant effects on mental health, enables individuals to seek out strategies and support that pave the way for a more fulfilling and balanced life. This chapter aims to equip readers with the knowledge to navigate the complexities of inattentive ADHD, emphasizing the importance of communication, accommodation, and self-care in the journey toward resilience and well-being.

# CHAPTER 4: UNDERSTANDING THE DIAGNOSIS OF ADULT INATTENTIVE ADHD

Diagnosing inattentive ADHD in adults often presents a complex challenge, subtly influencing daily life and remaining unnoticed for years. This chapter addresses the intricacies of recognizing this condition, the steps toward an accurate diagnosis, and the essential tools used in this critical process, with a special focus on understanding the socioeconomic impacts and providing resources for support.

## The Quiet Challenge of Inattentive ADHD

Inattentive ADHD often remains hidden, with its symptoms easily dismissed as personal quirks or misinterpreted as a lack of effort. The absence of hyperactive behavior means adults with this condition might not show the overt difficulties that prompt diagnosis in younger individuals. This lack of recognition, coupled with common myths that ADHD is a childhood disorder or solely about hyperactivity, leads to many adults being undiagnosed.

Crucial factors contributing to its underrecognition include:
- **Internalized Symptoms:** The core symptoms of inattentive ADHD, such as difficulty focusing and forgetfulness, are internal and not always visible to others.
- **Misconceptions and Myths:** Misunderstandings about what ADHD encompasses can prevent adults from realizing they may have the condition.

# Unseen and Unheard: Recognizing Adult Inattentive ADHD

- **Overlap with Other Conditions:** Inattentive ADHD's symptoms can resemble those of other mental health issues, complicating diagnosis.

## The Journey to Diagnosis

Getting a diagnosis of inattentive ADHD involves a detailed assessment by healthcare professionals. Adults recognizing symptoms in themselves is the first step, followed by seeking help from specialists. This process is thorough, with clinicians gathering a comprehensive understanding of the individual's symptoms, their impact over time, and any family history of ADHD.

Steps include:
- **Initial Discussions:** Sharing experiences, challenges, and medical history with a healthcare provider.
- **Detailed Assessments:** Utilizing psychological evaluations and questionnaires to construct a broad view of the individual's condition.
- **Exclusion of Other Conditions:** Screening for other mental health disorders or medical issues that could mimic ADHD symptoms.

## Tools for Diagnosis

A variety of diagnostic tools are employed to help identify adult inattentive ADHD, each offering a structured way to capture the individual's experiences and the extent of their symptoms.

Important tools used in diagnosis:
- **Adult ADHD Self-Report Scale (ASRS):** A questionnaire that helps articulate symptoms of inattentive ADHD.
- **Structured Clinical Interviews:** These conversations assess ADHD symptoms systematically.
- **Behavioral Checklists:** Insights from the individual and feedback from close contacts provide a rounded perspective on symptom manifestation.
- **Cognitive Testing:** Identifies cognitive patterns associated with ADHD, supporting a comprehensive diagnosis.

## Unseen and Unheard: Recognizing Adult Inattentive ADHD

<u>Socioeconomic Impacts and Support</u>

For many adults with inattentive type ADHD, maintaining steady employment can be challenging, often leading to financial instability. Recognizing this, it's important to highlight that individuals with inattentive ADHD may face socioeconomic hurdles, including lower income due to employment challenges.

Resources for support include:
- **Local Mental Health Services:** Many communities offer sliding-scale fees based on income, providing affordable access to therapy and counseling.
- **ADHD Support Organizations:** Groups such as CHADD (Children and Adults with Attention-Deficit/Hyperactivity Disorder) offer resources, support groups, and guidance on navigating ADHD, including financial assistance programs.
- **Government Assistance Programs:** Programs like Medicaid may provide healthcare support for those meeting low-income criteria. Additionally, vocational rehabilitation services can offer job training and placement assistance.
- **Online Resources:** Websites and forums dedicated to ADHD provide valuable information, strategies for management, and community support that can be accessed from anywhere.

Understanding the path to diagnosing adult inattentive ADHD, with an awareness of its broader life impacts, is crucial. This chapter aims not only to guide individuals through the diagnosis process but also to acknowledge the economic challenges faced and to offer a starting point for finding help and building a supportive network. Remember, reaching out for a diagnosis is a significant step towards gaining insight, accessing treatment, and enhancing overall quality of life amidst the challenges of ADHD.

# CHAPTER 5: MOVING FORWARD WITH INATTENTIVE ADHD

Discovering that inattentive ADHD is at the root of long-standing personal challenges can feel like a breakthrough, offering clarity and direction for the journey ahead. This chapter aims to guide you through the next steps, highlighting effective treatments, lifestyle adjustments, and the value of seeking professional advice to manage this condition with confidence and resilience.

## Exploring Treatment Pathways

Treating inattentive ADHD in adults requires a personalized approach, combining various strategies to address each individual's unique situation and needs.

- **Medication:** Often a cornerstone of treatment, stimulant and non-stimulant medications can greatly improve focus and control impulsivity. It's important to view medication as one component of a comprehensive plan, tailored with professional guidance to suit your needs.
- **Cognitive Behavioral Therapy (CBT):** This therapy is a powerful tool for adults with ADHD, helping to modify unhelpful thinking patterns, enhance organizational abilities, and navigate daily challenges. CBT is also effective for addressing any accompanying anxiety or depression.
- **Coaching:** ADHD coaching offers practical support in managing daily tasks, setting achievable goals, and using one's strengths to overcome difficulties. A coach can provide personalized strategies and encouragement to navigate the complexities of ADHD.

## Making Lifestyle Adjustments

Adopting certain lifestyle changes and coping mechanisms can significantly boost treatment outcomes and enhance quality of life.

- **Building a Routine:** A structured daily schedule can mitigate common symptoms like forgetfulness and disorganization. Employing planners, reminder apps, and alarms are practical ways to enhance task management and time awareness.
- **Practicing Mindfulness and Staying Active:** Engaging in mindfulness exercises and regular physical activity can sharpen focus, reduce impulsivity, and elevate mood. These practices support overall well-being and cognitive health.
- **Optimizing Diet and Sleep:** A nutritious diet and consistent sleep patterns are foundational for managing ADHD symptoms effectively. Tailoring these aspects of your lifestyle can lead to noticeable improvements in daily functioning.

## Professional Support and Community

Crafting a path through the world with inattentive ADHD often involves a team of supportive professionals and a network of individuals who understand what you're going through.

- **Finding Skilled Professionals:** Seek out healthcare providers with expertise in adult ADHD. Recommendations from primary care physicians, mental health professionals, or ADHD support organizations can be highly valuable.
- **Developing a Tailored Treatment Plan:** Work closely with your healthcare team to create a dynamic treatment plan that reflects your specific challenges, preferences, and objectives. This collaborative approach ensures that your plan remains relevant and supportive as your journey unfolds.
- **Connecting with Others:** Participating in support groups and online forums can offer camaraderie, insights, and practical advice from people who truly get it. These connections can be a rich source of comfort and motivation.

## Embracing the Process

For those managing on a limited income, finding affordable treatment options and support is crucial. Community health centers, patient assistance programs for medications, sliding scale therapy services, and online resources can provide accessible care and information. Additionally, many ADHD support organizations offer resources specifically designed to help those facing financial constraints.

Understanding your ADHD is a significant first step, but remember, it's okay to feel overwhelmed by the prospect of what comes next. Take things one step at a time, focusing on small, manageable steps forward. Every effort counts, and progress, no matter how incremental, is still progress. This chapter is here to remind you that with the right strategies, support, and mindset, navigating life with inattentive ADHD can lead to a fulfilling and empowered existence.

# CONCLUSION: WALKING YOUR UNIQUE PATH WITH ADULT INATTENTIVE ADHD

As we wrap up "Unseen and Unheard: Recognizing Adult Inattentive ADHD," let's acknowledge a vital truth: navigating life with ADHD is a deeply personal and continuous journey. It's not about fixing something that's wrong with you; it's about embracing your unique perspective and finding the tools and techniques that help you thrive.

### Awareness and Self-Acceptance: The Cornerstones of Growth

The journey begins with awareness. Realizing that inattentive ADHD plays a role in your life isn't a mark of defeat; it's a crucial step towards a richer, more satisfying experience. Self-acceptance follows, allowing you to view yourself more compassionately, understanding that ADHD is a part of your story but not the entirety of it. Remember, you're not at fault for having ADHD. It's a neurological condition that, with the right support, can be navigated successfully.

### Your Journey: Celebrating Each Step

Adopting a "step by step" mentality underscores the importance of progress, no matter the size. Every effort you make to understand and manage your ADHD is significant. Revel in the small victories, whether it's sticking to a schedule or tackling a long-avoided task. These triumphs fuel your journey forward, building confidence along the way.
here. Insert chapter six text here. Insert chapter six text here. Insert chapter six text here. Insert chapter six text here. Insert chapter six text here. Insert chapter six text here. Insert chapter six text here. Insert chapter six text here. Insert chapter six text here. Insert chapter six text here. Insert chapter six text here. Insert chapter six text here. Insert chapter six text here. Insert chapter six text here. Insert 20 Small Actions to Enhance Your Day

# Unseen and Unheard: Recognizing Adult Inattentive ADHD

1. Place **sticky notes** in strategic spots as task reminders.
2. Set **multiple alarms** for your various commitments.
3. Break tasks into bite-sized steps with **lists**.
4. **Declutter** your space regularly to minimize distractions.
5. Organize your day with a **planner**.
6. **Prioritize** tasks based on urgency.
7. Incorporate **breaks** to sustain focus.
8. Designate a **quiet workspace** to limit distractions.
9. **Exercise** to boost mental clarity.
10. Engage in **mindfulness** for focus and stress reduction.
11. Establish **routines** to streamline your day.
12. **Reach out** for support from your network.
13. Practice saying **no** to safeguard your time.
14. Utilize **apps** for organization.
15. Simplify meals with **prep** ahead of time.
16. Ensure a consistent **sleep schedule**.
17. **Delegate** tasks when you can.
18. Set **achievable goals** to prevent overwhelm.
19. **Celebrate** your progress and resilience.
20. Embrace **self-compassion**; be gentle with yourself.

## Finding Support: A Guide for Everyone

If you're beginning to explore the possibility of adult inattentive ADHD, here's a simplified guide, especially tailored for those without health insurance or with limited incomes:

1. **Reflect** on your symptoms and their impact on your life.
2. **Learn** about ADHD, with a focus on adult inattentive type.
3. **Consult** a healthcare professional, even if it means reaching out to community health centers or clinics that offer services based on income.
4. **Seek referrals** to ADHD specialists or mental health professionals; these can sometimes be obtained through community services at no cost.
5. **Undergo evaluation** for a comprehensive understanding of your situation.
6. **Explore diagnosis and treatment options**, including affordable medication programs, therapy, and lifestyle adjustments.
7. **Educate** yourself continuously about ADHD.
8. **Connect** with support groups and online communities.
9. **Review** and adjust your treatment plan regularly.
10. **Prioritize self-care**, focusing on practices that enhance both mental and physical well-being.

For those needing insurance, remember that low-cost or even free options may be available through Healthcare.gov, providing a valuable resource for accessing necessary support and treatment.

Embracing life with adult inattentive ADHD involves getting to know yourself better, making adjustments big and small, and reaching out for support. Remember, every step forward, no matter how modest, is a step towards a life where you can flourish. You're not journeying alone, and every effort you make paves the way to a more manageable, rewarding existence.

## ABOUT THE AUTHOR

My journey to understanding myself took a pivotal turn at the age of 45 when I was diagnosed with adult inattentive type ADHD. For decades, I wandered through life under the heavy cloud of misunderstanding, labeling myself a failure without knowing the real challenge I was facing. This lack of awareness about adult inattentive ADHD and its impact led to strained relationships with friends, family, significant others, and even my three children. The narrative of my life was one of constant struggle, trying to piece together why I felt so out of sync with the world around me.

The turning point came unexpectedly, through the keen observation of one of my children during her high school years. She saw through the veil of my struggles and recognized symptoms that had gone unnoticed for so long. This was the catalyst for change, the moment that set me on a path toward self-discovery and management of my condition. I began weekly therapy sessions through an organization offering support for those with limited incomes, a resource that became my beacon of hope.

Therapy opened my eyes to the reality of living with inattentive ADHD, equipping me with strategies and insights to navigate daily life more effectively. Medication, specifically stimulants, has played a crucial role in managing my symptoms, helping me to focus and maintain a semblance of balance in my hectic world.

Despite the challenges, I've managed to maintain my current job for over four years, relying on a combination of part-time roles to meet my financial needs. Sticky notes have become more than just a tool; they're my lifeline, a simple yet powerful way to keep my day structured and my tasks in view.

Financial stability remains a struggle, but I'm slowly finding my footing. I've learned to take life one day at a time, breaking down overwhelming challenges into manageable pieces, sometimes even taking it one hour at a time when the day feels too daunting.

My story is one of late diagnosis, self-acceptance, and ongoing adaptation. It's a testament to the fact that understanding and support can transform lives, even when they come later than we hope. My journey is far from over, but with each step, I'm learning to navigate my world with newfound clarity and purpose.

I have been trying to write about this subject for about 2 years. Without the help of AI this project would have never gotten done. I have started this project about three times. I am not doing this series to make money. I am doing it because if I would have had this information I would be so much better off both mentally and financially. I just want to help people.

Printed in Great Britain
by Amazon